SO-BRO-895

IMAGES
of America

MEDFORD

The Medford High School Baseball Team in 1958 included, from left to right: (front row) M. Franceschi, A. MacMillan, J. DiMatteo, S. Lentine, P. Hogan, O. Veitch, F. DiAngelis, L. Perella, and B. Celino; (back row) B. Caluani, D. Bucci, B. Curtin, J. Silverio, D. DelGaudio, V. Garo, W. Poffenberger, R. Black, L. White, D. Dalton, Manager Leonard Colasanti, and Coach Arthur Terrill. (Courtesy of the Medford Public Library.)

IMAGES
of America

MEDFORD

Anthony Mitchell Sammarco

ARCADIA

SOUTH BOSTON

Published by Arcadia Publishing,
an imprint of Tempus Publishing, Inc.
2 Cumberland Street
Charleston, SC 29401

Printed in Great Britain.

Library of Congress Catalog Card Number: 98-88698

For all general information contact Arcadia Publishing at:
Telephone 843-853-2070
Fax 843-853-0044
E-Mail arcadia@charleston.net

For customer service and orders:
Toll-Free 1-888-313-BOOK

Visit us on the internet at http://www.arcadiaimages.com

In Honor of My Parents
Anthony Sammarco and Mary T. Mitchell Sammarco

The Medford High School Basketball Team in 1958 included, from left to right: (front row) J. Foti, P. Jenney, S. Shiff, Captain Robert LeBert, T. Rose, A. De Leo, and J. Galloway; (middle row) Coach J. Walter Langley, T. McMasters, D. Pratt, J. Poole, A. Lucey, Manager David Amundsen, J. Sarnie, J. Pietrantoni, A. Riley, and J. Bernard; (back row) L. Perella, J. Hurley, G. Davis, A. Foti, R. Martin, R. Rappolo, R. Walsh, and P. Gagne. (Courtesy of the Medford Public Library.)

CONTENTS

City of Medford

Office of The Mayor
Rooms 202-204, City Hall
Medford, Massachusetts 02155
Telephone (781) 393-2408

MICHAEL J. MCGLYNN
MAYOR

FAX (781) 393-2514
TDD (781) 393-2516

Dear Readers,

Welcome to the City of Medford, Massachusetts, located 5 miles north of Boston. Medford has a long and proud history, dating back to 1630, as of the oldest settlements in North America. It was made famous for its "Clipper Ships", "Medford Crackers" and "Medford Rum". It was incorporated a City in 1892.

The Christmas Song, "Jingle Bells" was authored here, and Fannie Farmer wrote her famous cookbooks here. George Washington planned Revolutionary War strategy here, and Paul Revere awoke Medford residents to the call, "the British are coming". Prince Hall and Lydia Maria Child were residents who fought to end slavery. Massachusetts Governor John Brooks was born here and aviator Amelia Earhardt resided here. It is important that we protect and preserve our heritage for all future generations.

Medford, is primarily a residential community, comprised of distinct neighborhoods bonded together by common good will. As Mayor, I am committed to promoting a healthy and attractive environment for all our citizens. It is my hope that you will find this book about Medford interesting and informative. If you should decide to visit and/or to make Medford your home, please come by and introduce yourself...we look forward to welcoming you.

Sincerely,

MICHAEL J. McGLYNN, MAYOR

INTRODUCTION

Settled in 1630, Medford was described in Wood's *New England Prospect* nine years later as being "three miles from Charlestown by land, and a league and a half by water. It is seated by the water-side very pleasantly . . . [and] at the head of the river are great and spacious ponds, wither the alewives press to spawn." The settlement upon the Mystic River, originally referred to as Meadford, was headed by Governor Matthew Craddock, who ironically never visited Medford, and was a flourishing village with farms, fisheries, and shipbuilding—the *Blessing of the Bay* was launched in 1631 by Governor John Winthrop. Known as a "peculiar town," Medford was not actually a town but a plantation personally owned by Governor Craddock. Though settled in 1630, Medford would have no place of worship until 1690, when Harvard students ministered to the residents, nor a school until 1719 when Henry Davidson was hired as the first school teacher. The population remained low, with only 230 residents living in Medford in 1701.

A small town for the first two centuries after it was settled, Medford was only a few miles from Boston; the ford across the Mystic River at the rear of what is now the Medford Co-Operative Bank was built in 1637 as a toll road and all who crossed to the north had to pay this levy—which remained in effect until 1787. This transportation through the town was later augmented in the early 19th century with convenient roads such as the Medford Turnpike (now Mystic Avenue) and the Middlesex Canal that connected Boston and Lowell, allowing transportation to thrive. Though the canal, which was laid through Medford in 1803 and connected Charlestown and Lowell, was superseded by the Boston and Lowell Railroad in 1835, it was an important means of transporting goods from Boston and had a desirable effect on the local economy. By 1840, Medford had four places of worship, a Congregational, Unitarian, Universalist, and Methodist church. It would not be until 1855 that Roman Catholics began worshipping in Craddock's "peculiar" plantation. The farms had begun to give way to such developments as the Boston and Lowell Railroad in 1835, the Medford Railroad which connected Medford Square with the Boston and Maine Line in 1845, the Lawrence Rum Distillery, shipbuilding establishments, and numerous brick manufactories. The shipbuilding concerns along Ship Street (now Riverside Avenue) in Medford were one of its greatest, and most prolific attractions, with over 500 vessels with a combined tonnage of 230,000 tons being built in the first five decades of the 19th century.

By the time of the Civil War, Medford's population had increased to 10,000. A small, but conveniently situated town, it was to attract numerous new residents by the late 19th and early

20th centuries with the ease of travel by both railroad and streetcars. With such natural scenic spots as the Middlesex Fells, Spot and Wright Ponds, and the bucolic Mystic River which flowed through the town and connected Wellington and West Medford, it was just a matter of time before the town would vote to incorporate itself, which it did in 1892, as the city of Medford. After that time, it seemed as if Medford was to become one of the most popular places of residence in the metropolitan Boston area. Serviced by horse-drawn streetcars and the Boston and Lowell Railroad before 1870, these modes of transportation were soon superseded by electric streetcars and later, buses that eased transportation problems from Sullivan Square and Harvard Stations. With the extension of the Orange Line of the "T" in the 1970s, Wellington Station became a major transit point between Boston and Medford.

Medford was to share with its neighboring town Somerville the founding in 1852 of Tufts College, established as an Universalist institution and situated on College (formerly Walnut) Hill in the Hillside section of the town. The land for the college was donated by Charles Tufts of Somerville, who when asked what he was going to do with his land said he "would put a light on the hill," and the college was eventually to straddle both sides of that hill with its own depot on the Boston and Lowell Railroad Line. Today, Tufts University is a leading school in the country, and an important feature in Medford.

By the turn of the 20th century, Medford's population had increased to 18,244 residents. The city form of government had been adopted in 1892 (by a close vote of 382 to 342 votes), and the first mayor was General Samuel Crocker Lawrence, whose estate would eventually be subdivided for the Lawrence Estates. The new city would see tremendous changes over the next century. As these changes were taking place so quickly, residents began to lobby for the protection of the Fells, and much of the open land in north Medford was designated in 1895 the Middlesex Fells Reservation, with scenic vista, ponds, and nature trails. By the time of the Great Depression, Medford had become a city of residents who came from all parts of the world; between World War I and World War II, Medford's population swelled to just under 60,000 residents, with hundreds of new houses being built from the Hillside to Fulton Heights and from Wellington to South Medford—all to house the influx of new residents. The new citizens of Medford were to come from adjoining cities and towns as well as from all parts of Europe—all striving to make a better life for their families, and in the process broadening Medford's capabilities and resources. This cosmopolitan aspect was reflected in the grocery stores, fruit vendors, and bakeries in the city—each offering exotic and unusual items. This strong aspect of diversity continues to this day, making Medford not the average bedroom community of Boston but one of the finest residential communities in metropolitan Boston.

One
EARLY MEDFORD

Peter Tufts (1617–1700) built this house c. 1677. Today it is among the oldest brick houses in this country. Built of locally made bricks, with a gambrel roof and unique oval windows, the house was one of few east of Medford Square in the years prior to the 19th century. Purchased and restored in the late 19th century by Samuel C. Lawrence, it is an important example of 17th-century construction that combines west country framing and the early aspect of Georgian design.

Looking east on Salem Street from Medford Square in the mid-19th century, one can see that the road was uneven and far less busy than today. On the right is the brick wall protecting the burial ground that had been laid out in 1683, with the Baptist church being seen beyond it. On the left is Dr. Mills's house, and just beyond is the Methodist church. Notice how uneven Salem Street was in the mid-19th century. (Courtesy of the Medford Public Library.)

The Fountain House was built in 1713 on Salem Street for use as a tavern. Named for the painted sign board depicting a fountain pouring punch into a large bowl, this tavern was a popular stop on the thoroughfare between Salem and Boston. The Fountain House was demolished in 1887. Its former site is now just west of Interstate 93, and is marked by an historical marker. (Courtesy of the Medford Public Library.)

The Simon Tufts House was built in 1709 at the western corner of High and Forest Streets. A three-story house with a lean-to in the rear, it was the home of the town doctor; the house was later used as the first location of the Medford Reading Room. (Courtesy of the Medford Public Library.)

Looking west from Medford Square, High Street in the mid-19th century was lined with stately trees. From the corner of Forest Street on the right are an oyster house and Simpson's Tavern, the old post office, and the Governor Brooks House.

The Thomas Seccomb House was built in 1756 on High Street, just west of Forest Street. Thomas Seccomb (1711–1773) was the son of Peter and Hannah Willis Seccomb, and with his wife Rebecca, he established in 1774 the Seccomb Fund which benefited the poor of Medford. On the right between the two houses can be seen the house of Daniel Lawrence on Forest Street. (Courtesy of the Medford Public Library.)

The Jonathan Wade House, known as the Old Garrison House, was a brick house built c. 1689 on Bradlee Road, just north of High Street. Though now it sits on a much smaller lot than it originally did, the house was built of Medford bricks and massive paired end chimneys. Jonathan Wade (1637–1689) married Deborah Dudley, and they were among the wealthiest residents in Medford in the 17th century. (Courtesy of the Medford Public Library.)

The Hall Houses on High Street created an impressive example of colonial houses built by the same family within one block. The Hall House, on the right, was built c. 1720 and was the home of Captain Isaac Hall (1739–1789) of the Medford Minute Men. Paul Revere stopped here on his midnight ride to alert Hall of the British march to Lexington; today it is the Gaffey Funeral Home, located at the corner of High and Bradlee Road. (Courtesy of the Medford Public Library.)

Major General (Doctor) John Brooks (1752–1825) was a noted physician in Medford who served in the Continental Army during the Revolution. Brooks served as governor of Massachusetts from 1816 to 1823. His monument in the Salem Street Burying Ground is a monumental granite obelisk in the center of the grounds.

Dr. Daniel Swan (1781–1864) was a noted medical practitioner of homeopathy, and an advocate of the health-preserving potency of sunshine. His house was just beyond the Hall Houses on High Street, just about where Governor's Avenue was laid out in 1892. The cupola of the second Medford High School can be seen on the left, rising just above the gambrel roof of the Richard Hall House. (Courtesy of the Medford Public Library.)

The Richard Hall House was located at 77 High Street, next to the second Medford High School (the Central School). This is now the site of the CVS Pharmacy on High Street; on the right can be seen Governor's Avenue, which had been laid out in 1892. (Courtesy of the Medford Public Library.)

The Jonathan Watson House was at 153 High Street, to the left of the First Unitarian Church, which was at the corner of Powderhouse Road. General George Washington was entertained here in 1789 when breakfast was served to him. Notice the driveway and granite balusters to the First Unitarian Church. (Courtesy of the Medford Public Library.)

The Train House was next to the Watson House. In the rear, the Ell was built in 1771 and used as the second schoolhouse in town. Traincroft Road, which runs behind this house from Rural Avenue to Powderhouse Road, perpetuates the name of the Train family. (Courtesy of the Medford Public Library.)

The Reverend Ebenezer Turell House was at the corner of High Street and Rural Avenue. The stone wall survives, though Traincroft Road was cut through and huge stone slabs placed on piers to either side of the road. (Courtesy of the Medford Public Library.)

Reverent Ebenezer Turell (1701–1778) was the second minister of the First Parish, Medford, which had been settled in 1724; his portrait was painted in 1734 by John Smibert, a Colonial artist and designer of the 1742 Faneuil Hall in Boston. Turell preached more than 5,000 sermons and baptized over 1,000 persons during his term as pastor. (Collection of The Newark Museum, Newark, New Jersey.)

The Jonathan Brooks House was built *c*. 1781 and is located at the corner of High and Woburn Streets. High Street led to West Medford and Menotomy (West Cambridge) and Woburn Street to Woburn. On the left can be seen the Reverend Charles Brooks House. (Courtesy of the Medford Public Library.)

The Ensign John Bradshaw House was built *c*. 1710 and still stands at the corner of High Street and Hasting's Lane. The site of this house was used as Medford's first meetinghouse, and here the first church was organized in 1713. (Courtesy of the Medford Public Library.)

The Thatcher Magoun Mansion was designed by Asher Benjamin (1773–1845) and was built on High Street, at the present corner of High Street and Boynton Road. An elegant Greek Revival house with double swell bays and monumental Ionic columns, it was testimony to Magoun's acumen as a successful shipbuilder. Thatcher Magoun Jr. donated his father's mansion to the town for use as the Medford Public Library. (Courtesy of the Medford Public Library.)

Abraham Touro (1777–1822) was a resident of Medford, but his philanthropy extended to many charities, among them the founding of the Massachusetts General Hospital and the Touro Synagogue in Newport, Rhode Island. Touro Avenue perpetuates his name in Medford. (Courtesy of the Medford Public Library.)

Susanna Haswell Rowson (1762–1824) was a noted educator who kept a young ladies' academy on the Timothy Bigelow Estate from 1799 to 1803. A popular author, she penned the immensely popular novel *Charlotte Temple* in 1791. An actress turned educator, she was famous in her own time for her education for young ladies.

Lydia Maria Francis Child (1802–1880) was the daughter of David and Susannah Reed Francis, whose house was at the corner of Salem and Ashland Streets. A noted author, her book *An Appeal in Behalf of that Class of Americans called Africans* would thrust her into the limelight of the anti-slavery cause and make her writings unpopular due to her radical views. Her most famous poem was *Over the river and through the woods to grandfather's house we go*, which has become beloved to generations as the ideal for a family reunion during Thanksgiving.

The Peter Chardon Brooks House was built in 1805 in West Medford near the Middlesex Canal. The mansion was demolished in 1913. (Courtesy of the Medford Historical Society.)

Peter Chardon Brooks the second (1798–1880) was a merchant in the firm of Sargeant & Brooks. His family owned extensive tracts of land in West Medford, which at one time wished to secede from the town and incorporate itself as the town of Brooks.

Reverend Charles Brooks (1795–1872) is considered the father of the Normal School. He wrote *A History of the Town of Medford*, published in 1855. Brooks devoted his life to scientific studies but after his eyesight began to fail, he turned his attention to the founding of a society for the relief of aged and destitute clergymen.

The Reverend Charles Brooks House is located on High Street, just west of Woburn Street.

The Angier-Boynton House was built in 1842 at the corner of High Street and Boynton Road for John and Abigail Adams Angier. A Gothic Revival house designed by Alexander Jackson Davis, its crenelation and decorative barge boards have been removed but the house is still an architecturally important example of Davis's interpretation of Gothicism. (Courtesy of the Medford Public Library.)

The Thatcher Magoun Jr. House was a winter wonderland in this c. 1875 photograph.

The Thatcher Magoun Jr. Mansion was an impressive Italianate house with rusticated sides and corner quoining. The projecting tower had windows on all four sides, allowing panoramic views over the Mystic River and of Medford. The marble statues in the foreground were later purchased by Isabella Stewart Gardner for her new house in Boston, Fenway Court. (Courtesy of the Medford Public Library.)

Looking towards High Street from the south bank of the Mystic River about 1890, the spire of the First Unitarian Church at the corner of High Street and Powderhouse Road rises above the Magoun Mansion. On the far left can be seen the spire of Grace Episcopal Church, the only identifiable landmark standing today, with the Medford Christian Science Church next to it. Notice the hay rick on the bank of the Mystic River on the lower left. (Courtesy of the Medford Public Library.)

The Stearns House was built in 1845 and was located on a large estate between Main Street and College Avenue in South Medford. In the two decades before 1863, this house was a stop on the Underground Railroad for runaway slaves from the South seeking freedom in the North and Canada. Eventually Stearns, Stanley, and Frederick Avenues would be cut through the estate in the early 20th century. (Courtesy of the Medford Public Library.)

Mary Preston Stearns (Mrs. George L. Stearns) poses for her photograph in her garden in the mid-19th century. An avid gardener, she was an early member of the Massachusetts Horticultural Society and maintained a lavish estate with gardens and orchards in South Medford.

George Luther Stearns (1809–1867) was an ardent abolitionist, financially supporting the anti-slavery cause for many years. A wealthy manufacturer of lead pipe and sheet lead, he directed much of his profits towards the raising of the 54th Regiment and the 55th Regiment, two companies composed of African Americans who fought in the Union Army during the Civil War. His friendship with John Brown and his harboring of runaway slaves showed his abolitionist forthrightness.

A man walks along College Avenue in 1889. Named for Tufts College, College Avenue was a bucolic country road lined with mature shade trees in the late 19th century. (Courtesy of the Medford Historical Society.)

The Royall Family was painted in 1741 by the Colonial artist Robert Feke. From left to right are: Penelope Royall Vassall (1724–1800), Mary McIntosh Palmer (the sister of Mrs. Royall), Elizabeth Royall (1740–1747), Elizabeth McIntosh Borland Royall (1722–1770), and Isaac Royall Jr. (1719–1781). (Collection of Harvard Law School.)

The west facade of the Royall House was its principal facade. The wood was scored to imitate stone rustication and the entrance was flanked by Ionic pilasters. Guest would be driven along the carriage path (now George Street) and their carriage would pull up to a cobblestoned courtyard, with the garden and summerhouse just beyond the house.

Two

THE ROYALL HOUSE

The Royall House was once set on an extensive estate of over 500 acres that was known as Ten Hills Farm. Built by the Usher Family, the house was purchased by Isaac Royall Sr. (1677–1739) in 1732 and remodeled into a three-story mansion fit for an aristocrat. Royall's wealth was derived from sugar plantations on Antigua in the West Indies, allowing him to lavish money on what was considered the finest mansion in Colonial New England. (Courtesy of the Medford Public Library.)

A c. 1885 photograph shows the Royall House while occupied by the Tidd family, who built an ell on the right to house their large number of children and grandchildren. The east facade had corner quoining with wooden aprons beneath the windows, a marked difference from the rusticated west facade.

The Royalls brought 27 slaves from their sugar plantation on Antigua to run their new estate in Medford in 1737. This building, part brick and part wood clapboard, is today the only remaining example of slave quarters that survive in New England. In 1754, the slaves living here included Joseph, Plato, Phoebe, Peter, Abraham, Cooper, Stephy, George, Hagar, Mira, Nancy, and Betsy. In 1765, there were 49 slaves in various households in Medford.

Isaac Royall Jr. (1719–1781) was painted by John Singleton Copley. (Collection of the Boston Museum of Fine Arts.)

Elizabeth McIntosh Royall (1722–1770) was painted by John Singleton Copley. (Collection of The Virginia Museum, Richmond, Virginia.)

The West Parlor of the Royall House had elegantly carved woodwork with arched openings flanking the fireplace. A copy of Royall's portrait by Feke hangs above the fireplace.

The Marble Chamber was the principal bedroom on the second floor, directly above the West Parlor. The Corinthian pilasters flanking the fireplace were marbleized and the original wall hangings were of leather painted in China.

Mary McIntosh Royall (1744–1786) and Elizabeth Royall (1747–1775), with their pet bird and lap dog, were painted in 1757 by John Singleton Copley. (Collection of the Boston Museum of Fine Arts.)

The Summerhouse on the Royall Estate was an octagonal structure that was surmounted by a carved statue of Mercury. Once the site of the courtships of the Royall daughters, Mary by the Honorable John Erving and Elizabeth by Sir William Pepperell, the structure eventually succumbed to time and only one section of the octagonal house survives and is today a decoration in the garden. (Courtesy of the Medford Public Library.)

The Royall House was purchased by an association in 1905 to preserve it from further decay. To raise funds for its restoration, *The Pageant of the Royall House* was presented in 1915. Written by Ruth Dame Coolidge, the history of the house came to life. Here, the Dance of the Spirits of Fells, Meadow, and River dance in front of the West Facade. Dancing the Spirit of the House was Ruth Lawrence and her co-spirits were Louise Taylor, Mildred Brooks, Beatrice Towne, Winifred Hernan, Marjorie Brown, Mary Appleton, Louise Glidden, Elva Nevons, Helen Caulkins, Ruth Isley, Margaret Eeles, Catherine Clough, Eleanor and Ruth Albee, Grace Wilkerson, Doris Pierce, Ruth Saunders, Marion Hervey, Marjorie Preston, and Alice Norton. (Courtesy of the Medford Public Library.)

A Colonial farm scene was presented by members of the Medford Women's Club and showed women spinning, carding wool, and churning. Participating were Mesdames Pickering, Brown, Weston, Tryon, Fenton, Harvey, Barnes, Young, Hamlin, Beaman, and Goodspeed. The children were Catherine Brown and Eleanor Reilly. (Courtesy of the Medford Public Library.)

The Dance of the Spirits of Hearth and Home, putting to Flight the Spirits of Snow, Wind, and Rain, was led by Ruth Lawrence. The dresses representing Hearth and Home were the brownish-grey of ashes and the red of flame; those of Snow, Wind, and Rain were blue with mantles of purple. (Courtesy of the Medford Public Library.)

The Spirits of Hearth and Home, clad in diaphanous gowns of pale green and pink with oak leaves entwined in their hair, are led into The Royall House by Ruth Lawrence. (Courtesy of the Medford Public Library.)

A Colonial tea was reenacted with aplomb during the 1905 pageant. (Courtesy of the Medford Public Library.)

In the segment "A Visit from Washington," General George Washington (played by Henry Van De Bogert Jr.) kisses the hand of Molly Stark (played by Mrs. Edward Hayes). During the Revolution, General Stark had been induced by Dr. Simon Tufts to use the Royall House as his headquarters, thereby saving it from harm. During his residence, he referred to the house as "Hobgobblin Hall." (Courtesy of the Medford Public Library.)

Three
THE CITY OF MEDFORD

A group of baseball players, with their manager, pose for a photograph about 1890. With "Medford" emblazoned on their uniforms, they represent the large increase in population in Medford, many of whom would attend baseball games. By the time it became a city in 1892, Medford's population was growing by leaps and bounds. (Courtesy of the Medford Historical Society.)

The seal of the city of Medford was adopted in 1892 and had a ship being built in the center of the seal. With the prosperity brought to Medford during the heyday of shipbuilding, it is appropriate that the rising sun shines upon this industry. On the left is the Tufts House on Riverside Avenue, and on the right the Bunker Hill Monument.

General Samuel Crocker Lawrence (1832–1911) was the first mayor of Medford. Owner of the Lawrence Distillery that produced world famous "Medford Rum," Lawrence was a successful businessman whose investments in insurance, railroads, and land in Medford made him one of the town's wealthiest residents. His estate was on Rural Avenue and after his wife's death, it was developed into the premier residential neighborhood, the "Lawrence Estates." (Courtesy of the Medford Public Library.)

Members of the Lawrence Light Guard, the local militia founded in 1854, pose in front of Medford Town Hall as they depart on April 19, 1861, for the Civil War. During the period between 1861 and 1865, 769 men served from Medford in the Civil War. The men were recruited at the town hall. (Courtesy of the Medford Public Library.)

The mayor and aldermen of the city of Medford posed for their photograph in 1905, the 275th anniversary of the founding of the town. From left to right are: (front row) aldermen Staples, Brewer, Monroe, Mayor Dwyer, aldermen Lovell, Pitman, and Weatherbee; (middle row) aldermen Geary, Minard, Roberts, Bacheller, Hanscom, Brown, and Wellington; (back row) aldermen Scott, Lewis, Daly, Enwright, Byram, and Crosby.

The Armory at 92 High Street was designed by Shepley, Rutan and Coolidge in 1901 and presented by Samuel Crocker Lawrence to the Veteran Association of the Lawrence Light Guard. An impressive rough-hammered granite building with crenelated towers, it had meeting rooms, offices, and a drill hall in the rear. Today, the former Armory is known as the Marcus Fonzi Professional Condominiums, which occupy the once cavernous building. (Courtesy of the Medford Public Library.)

Members of the Lawrence Light Guard pose in formation in front of the Armory as they depart for World War I. (Courtesy of the Medford Historical Society.)

The Medford Police Department was organized in 1870 with eight policemen, who patrolled the entire town. Here, at the turn of the century, members of the department pose on the steps of the former police headquarters at Main and Swan Streets. (Courtesy of the Medford Public Library.)

The Medford Police Headquarters was located at the corner of Main and Swan Streets, on the site of the old Admiral Vernon Tavern. An impressive brick Romanesque building, it was photographed in 1895. (Courtesy of the Medford Public Library.)

Members of the Mystic Hose Company, Number One pose in 1874 on High Street in front of the Central School, the present site of CVS Pharmacy. The officers of this company hold bouquets of roses and the firemen wear helmets and shirts emblazoned with "Hose 1." Notice

The J.W. Mitchell, Hose Number 3 was organized in 1872 and was located north of the Swan School on Park Street. (Courtesy of the Medford Public Library.)

the young boy, probably the son of one of the firemen, sitting atop the cylindrical hose winder. (Courtesy of the Medford Public Library.)

Mystic Hose Number One is shown in front of the Central School on High Street about 1881. (Courtesy of the Medford Public Library.)

The Medford Firehouse was built in 1880 at the corner of Main and South Streets and was photographed at the turn of the century. An impressive red brick firehouse, it was used until 1959, when it was demolished to allow for an off-ramp for the Mystic Valley Parkway. (Courtesy of the Medford Historical Society.)

Ladder Number One races down Main Street from Medford Square at the turn of the century. The driver is Edgar H. Babcock and his three side riders are Percy Hathaway, Dana Haskell, and Hugh Fraser. (Courtesy of the Medford Historical Society.)

Judson Hanson poses with Hose Number One on Forest Street, in front of the Medford High School, at the turn of the century. Built in 1890 by the Abbott Downing Company, this hose truck was the latest model a century ago. (Courtesy of the Medford Historical Society.)

Posing in front of the Old Firehouse in 1926 are: (on the left) Captain Morse, Lt. F. Meagher, Francis Vye, Joseph Nestor, Joe Lenox, Bill Chamberlain, Oliver Nicoll, Pat Manley, John Henson, and Earnest Pearson; (center) Department Chief Burton Harvey, Chief Thomas Qualey, and Department Chief John Qualey; (right) Captain F. Sampson, Lt. J. Plante, F. Bresnahan, E. Carlson, C. Calahan, George McDonald, John Malloy, Jim Chase, Warren Vass, and W. Dowd. (Courtesy of the Medford Historical Society.)

Posing in 1919 are, from left to right: J. Plante, Lt. H. Woodbridge, John Henson, Bernard Papkee, Captain A. Morse, Department Chief Burton Harvey, Chief Thomas Qualey, Clarence Thompson, F. Bresnahan, unknown, John Malloy, Captain Bradish, and Fred Meagher. (Courtesy of the Medford Historical Society.)

Posing in front of a 1930 General Motors truck at the Fire Headquarters at South and Main Streets are, from left to right: Chief Qualey, Captain Morse, F. Warner, Joe Nestor, Rosie Hassam, Hank Vye, Oliver Nicoll, and John Henson. (Courtesy of the Medford Public Library.)

Chief Bacon, on the right, and Captain Walker of the Medford Fire Department pose in a 1914 Knox at the corner of Harvard Avenue and Bower Street. Notice the bell mounted to the hood of the automobile—a cord would be pulled to alert one and all to get out of the way! (Courtesy of the Medford Public Library.)

Engine Five, a 1913 Knox, is parked in front of the firehouse at the corner of Medford and Albion Streets in South Medford. (Courtesy of the Medford Public Library.)

The Spring Street Fire House was a small gambrel-roofed building with a soaring tower that doubled as a hose drying space. Engine Number 4 can be seen parked in front of the doors about 1928. (Courtesy of the Medford Public Library.)

The first post office was established in 1797 in Medford, with Samuel Buel serving as postmaster until 1813. Here, postmen pose outside the old Medford Post Office on Riverside Avenue about 1900. The present post office on Forest Street was designed by Arthur L. Blakeslee and was built in 1937 of face brick with trim of Vermont marble. There are superb Works Progress Administration (WPA) murals decorating the interior of the post office. (Courtesy of the Medford Historical Society.)

Clerks sort the mail in the Medford Post Office about 1900. A second post office was opened in 1852, and the first postmaster of the post office at West Medford was James W. Sanford. (Courtesy of the Medford Historical Society.)

Frank W. Lovett moves the first shovelful of soil for the new West Medford Post Office on August 2, 1926. (Courtesy of the Medford Public Library.)

Turning the first shovelful of soil for the new Medford City Hall on March 17, 1936, is Mayor John J. Irwin. On the left are Michael A. Dyer, the architect of the new building, and John J. Kelliher, the contractor. (Courtesy of the Medford Public Library.)

The festivities of laying the cornerstone of the Medford City Hall on August 12, 1936, brought residents from every section of Medford to participate in this historic occasion. (Courtesy of the Medford Public Library.)

Medford City Hall was designed by Michael A. Dyer, a resident of Medford whose office was in Boston. The building was dedicated on September 11, 1937. A classical Georgian red brick building with Corinthian columns supporting a pediment, it presented an imposing addition to the former Medford Common. The cupola has a four-sided clock and a gilded dome that can be seen for miles.

This marble staircase, with bronze balustrades, leads from the first-floor entrance to the Rotunda. The first floor has walls of Travertine marble with inset panels and the second floor has richly ornamented cornices.

The Rotunda had an impressive coffered dome, with rosettes, supported by marble Corinthian columns. The doorway in the center leads to the Aldermanic Chamber, which occupies the second and third floors.

Four
MEDFORD SQUARE

Looking west from Medford Square up High Street in 1890, the small-town flavor of Medford is evident in this early Sunday morning photograph. The spire of Saint Joseph's Church rises on the left and the Medford Savings Bank punctuates the early 19th-century streetscape of High Street. The site of the old town pump has been replaced with a granite horse trough for thirsty horses passing through the square. (Courtesy of the Medford Public Library.)

A *c.* 1865 view of High Street shows a horse-drawn wagon being unloaded next to the Medford Town Hall. Designed by the noted architect Asher Benjamin (1774–1845) and built in 1833, the town hall had stores on the first floor and town offices and an assembly hall above. The Washington Hook & Ladder Company, chartered in 1829, was housed in the rear of the building.

The two duplex houses in the center were built in the 1840s and still stand today at 8 to 18 Salem Street, though one is covered in stucco and the other in vinyl siding, with both having been remodeled with stores opened on the first floor. The town pump can be seen in the foreground, with its own gas lamp for night pumping!

Looking east from Medford Square down Distill House Lane (now Riverside Avenue) in 1890, at the corner of Main Street is the Morgan Pharmacy and the specialty store of Yerxa and Yerxa. On the left is the bow-fronted Dodge Block that was rebuilt as the Macaulay Building, which now houses Papa Gino's. (Courtesy of the Medford Public Library.)

A streetcar passes through Medford Square from Salem Street headed south on Main Street to Sullivan Square. On the right is the old Medford Town Hall, which was built in 1833 and used for town, and later city, government until it was demolished in 1916. (Courtesy of the Medford Public Library.)

The Morgan Drug Store was located at the corner of Main Street and Distill House Lane (now Riverside Avenue.) Here, a gold-leafed mortar and pestle signifying a drugstore surmounts the support to the signboard of the Royal Oak Tavern, an 18th-century inn that was originally located on this site. Notice the distillery of the Lawrence family farther along on the left. (Courtesy of the Medford Public Library.)

Looking south along Main Street at Medford Square at the turn of the century, businesses were housed in various 18th- and early 19th-century buildings. The tall building with the cupola was the Boston and Maine Railroad depot. The only building to survive is the old brick grain storage warehouse on the right (with the fire escape) which now houses Dr. Zizza's office and the Medford Driving School. (Courtesy of the Medford Historical Society.)

Looking east on the Mystic River towards the Craddock Bridge about 1870, one can see the Carr & Page hardware store. The original bridge spanning the Mystic River was built in 1637, behind the present Medford Co-Operative Bank, and was referred to as the "Ford on the Mystic." (Courtesy of the Medford Public Library.)

The area between South and Summer Streets along Main Street was the site of the old Fire Station and the Medford House, an inn built in 1804 by Andrew Blanchard. A score of years ago it was the site of Carroll's Diner, a popular spot for dinner. (Courtesy of the Medford Public Library.)

Looking east on Salem Street from Medford Square, the turreted Bigelow Block is at the corner of Forest Street, with the spire of the Mystic Congregational Church visible. The bow-fronted brick block was the Dodge Block, which was replaced by the Macaulay Building. (Courtesy of the Medford Historical Society.)

Looking north on Forest Street about 1890, the Tufts Block is on the left and the Bigelow Block on the right. On Forest Street can be seen the Medford High School and on the right the facade of the Universalist Church. Oberholtzer, the Medford photographer, is seen crossing the street and Judge William Cushing Wait is standing on the far right. (Courtesy of the Medford Historical Society.)

P. Volpe & Sons fruit store was in the Bigelow Block at the turn of the century. Italians had begun to settle in Medford at the turn of the century and would exert a great influence on the city in the 20th century. Volpe's would close in 1950 after 65 years of providing quality fruits and vegetables to discriminating buyers. (Courtesy of the Medford Historical Society.)

For two centuries Medford Rum was distilled in the Hall-Lawrence Distillery on Distill House Lane (now Riverside Avenue). The distillery, located on "Distill House Lane"—that portion of the street between Main and Cross Streets—produced a fine, mellow rum that was made until 1905. On the right is the Richard Sprague House, which is at the corner of "Dead Man's Alley," the path that led to the Salem Street Burial Ground. (Courtesy of the Medford Historical Society.)

Near the old Medford Town Hall was the turreted Opera House. A large brick and brownstone building, it had stores on the first floor with a large hall for performances above. The Opera House suffered a fire in 1911 that destroyed the roof and turret, but two floors still remain with the Medford Optical Shop, Harmoney Supply, and the High Street Cafe located on the first floor. (Courtesy of the Medford Historical Society.)

Tufts Hall was built at the corner of High and Forest Streets, on the site of the Dr. Simon Tufts House. (Courtesy of the Medford Historical Society.)

The Medford Band poses for their photograph on Forest Street in 1876. The Medford Band was the result of the uniting of the Mystic Brass Band and the Cornet Band, which took place in 1873; in 1882 the band moved to Boston and was henceforth known as the Boston City Band. Tufts Hall can be seen on the left, and the Bigelow House, later the site of the Bigelow Building, on the right. (Courtesy of the Medford Public Library.)

The Lawrence Light Guard (founded in 1854 as Company E, Fifth Regiment) march down High Street on July 4, 1894. On the left can be seen the flag-draped city hall and the Opera House just beyond. On the right is the turreted Medford Savings Bank and the Hall Houses are just beyond. (Courtesy of the Medford Public Library.)

The Medford Savings Bank was organized in 1869 and was later located in this turreted brick building on High Street, between Bradlee Road and Brooks Lane. On the left can be seen the Captain Isaac Hall House, now Gaffey's Funeral Home. Notice the open land on the right which would be developed in the early 20th century. (Courtesy of the Medford Public Library.)

The Massachusetts Society of the Sons of the American Revolution (SAR) unveil a tablet to the memory of Governor John Brooks on June 16, 1906. Placed on the side of the Medford Savings Bank (the site of Brooks's house), it was later affixed to the Bradlee Road side of the present Medford Savings Bank.

Members of the Lawrence Light Guard march through Medford Square upon their return from World War I. The spire of Saint Joseph's Church can be seen in the distance, and on the right is the modern Tudor-Gothic office building (5 to 21 High Street) that replaced Tufts Hall and the Seccomb House. (Courtesy of the Medford Historical Society.)

The festivities really got under way by early afternoon when it seemed as if every resident of Medford turned out to welcome home the Lawrence Light Guard. Here, even streetcars are stopped on High Street due to the large number of jubilant residents. (Courtesy of the Medford Historical Society.)

The Craddock Bridge crossing the Mystic River was dismantled in 1880. The wooden bridge would eventually be replaced by a non-drawing stone bridge in 1882 that did not allow river traffic. In the distance is the first Saint Joseph's Church on High Street, now remodeled as Craddock's Apothecary Shop. (Courtesy of the Medford Public Library.)

The locks on the Mystic River seen to the left of the Craddock Bridge allowed for boats to pass. Looking west, the rear of the Lawrence Light Guard Armory can be seen on the right and a streetcar travels north on Main Street. (Courtesy of the Medford Public Library.)

Five

MEDFORD PUBLIC LIBRARY

The Medford Public Library was originally housed in the former Thatcher Magoun Mansion on High Street, the site of the present library since 1959. In 1875 the mansion was deeded to the Town of Medford by Thatcher Magoun Jr. for use as a public library; alterations were made to house an ever-increasing collection of books and papers. On the left can be seen the turn-of-the-century addition that had the "glass floors" that allowed light to penetrate the bookstacks. (Courtesy of the Medford Public Library.)

Thatcher Magoun (1775–1856) had noted architect Asher Benjamin design a magnificent Greek Revival mansion on High Street that was presented by his son to the Town of Medford in 1875 for the purpose of a library. With the donation of $1,000 for bookshelves by Thatcher Magoun Jr., seen at left, the former mansion was fitted for use by the library. The library had been founded in 1825 and was originally known as the Medford Social Library.

The circulation desk and stacks area in the old library was originally the Winter Parlor of the Magoun Mansion. The circular room had a discharge desk set into the wall, and the free-flying staircase to the second floor can be seen through the door on the left. A portrait of Thatcher Magoun, the builder of the mansion, hangs on the right. (Courtesy of the Medford Public Library.)

On the glass floor in the rear addition of the old library, Louise Feeley, assistant in the circulation department, marks books with an assistant preparing them for her. At the back desk is Edna McDonald. (Courtesy of the Medford Public Library.)

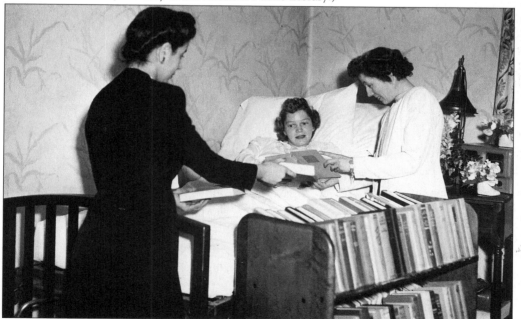

The Medford Public Library established a hospital branch in the early 1930s for patients at the Lawrence Memorial Hospital. Here two assistants offer reading material to a young lady at the hospital. The annual circulation of books at the hospital was 570 in 1931. (Courtesy of the Medford Public Library.)

A group of children admire a Christmas tree at the Salem Street Branch of the Medford Public Library in the 1950s. Seated at the desk is Harriet Bryden, the branch librarian. (Courtesy of the Medford Public Library.)

V. Kathleen James, branch librarian, and Priscilla Ryder assist patrons at the West Medford Branch of the Medford Public Library in the late 1940s. (Courtesy of the Medford Public Library.)

Two library assistants staff a deposit station at the West Medford Depot from the rear of a beach wagon during the summer of 1950. The West Medford Branch had been destroyed by fire in February 1950, so residents disembarking the train from Boston could browse through a selection of books there rather than travel to the library on High Street. (Courtesy of the Medford Public Library.)

At the Medford Library Centennial Evening Program on July 26, 1956, were, from left to right: City Manager James F. Shurtleff, Judge Lawrence G. Brooks, and Alfred Pompeo, mayor of Medford 1956–1957. (Courtesy of the Medford Public Library.)

To alleviate the overcrowded aspect of the library, a house adjacent to the Magoun Mansion was secured by the library trustees and used as the Childrens' Section. Built as a Queen Anne House at the corner of High Street and Hillside Avenue, it too was soon overcrowded. (Courtesy of the Medford Public Library.)

The crowded conditions of the library were not just in the Childrens' Room and the bookstacks. Here the librarian works at his desk in an office that was filled to overflowing with desks and chairs. Notice the large framed print above his rolltop desk that has historic scenes from around Medford. (Courtesy of the Medford Public Library.)

The city of Medford decided that a new, more modern library was an absolute necessity and the old Magoun Mansion was demolished to allow a new one to be built. Here, half the swell bay facade of the old library is gone, but the monumental Ionic columns still connote grandeur, even though they too would shortly fall. (Courtesy of the Medford Public Library.)

Demolition workers of the Framingham Building & Wrecking Company, with debris surrounding them on all sides, hold the wood sign, with gold-leafed letters of the Medford Public Library. (Courtesy of the Medford Public Library.)

Laying the cornerstone of the new library in 1958 is Helen G. Forsyth, librarian. Assisting in the ceremonies are, from left to right: John M. O'Loughlin, chairman of the Library's Board of Trustees, Judge Lawrence G. Brooks, Representative Alexander Cella, and Mrs. Sidney Olans, president of the Friends of the Malden Public Library. The new library was designed by Alderman and MacNeish of Springfield and was dedicated in 1960. (Courtesy of the Medford Public Library.)

In 1977, pieces of the Magoun Family silver were presented by members of the Conserva family to the library. From left to right are: Frank Levine, director of the Medford Public Library, Barbara Conserva, William Conserva, Mrs. Martin A. Conserva, Miss Barbara Conserva, and Mr. and Mrs William Conserva. Looking down upon this presentation is the portrait of Thatcher Magoun. (Courtesy of the Medford Public Library.)

Six

PLACES OF WORSHIP

The spire of Saint Joseph's Church rises just west of Medford Square on High Street. Built as the First Trinitarian Congregational Church, it was purchased in 1876 by the Catholic church and converted for use as the first Catholic church in Medford. Today, it still stands, though remodeled for use as Craddock's Apothecary Shop. On the left is the Medford Town Hall, a Greek Revival building designed by noted Boston architect Asher Benjamin and built in 1833 at the corner of High and Main Streets. (Courtesy of the Medford Public Library.)

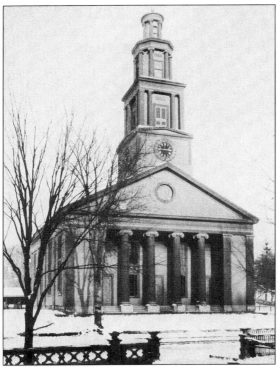

The First Unitarian Church was an impressive Greek Revival church designed by Asher Benjamin and built in 1839 at the corner of High Street and Powderhouse Road. An impressive church with monumental Ionic columns and a telescoping spire, it commanded one's attention on High Street until it was destroyed by fire in 1893. (Courtesy of the Medford Public Library.)

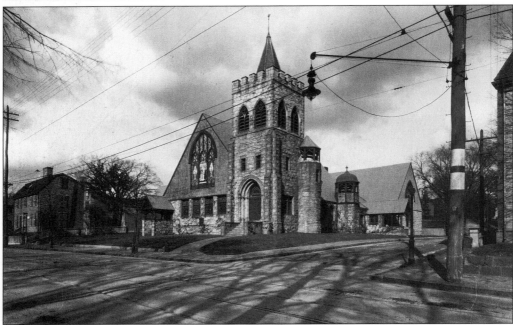

The Medford Unitarian Universalist Church was designed by J. Merrill Brown and built in 1894 at the corner of High Street and Powderhouse Road. An eclectic use of both Shingle Style design with Gothic details, the crenelated tower of this church is an impressive part of its design. On the left is the Jonathan Watson House. (Courtesy of the Medford Public Library.)

The earliest known photograph of the Grace Episcopal Church shows it set back from High Street with a fanciful wood fence along the street. Designed in 1867 by noted architect H.H. Richardson and donated by Mrs. Gorham Brooks, it was among Richardson's earliest commissions. The first rector of the church was Reverend David Haskins. (Courtesy of the Medford Historical Society.)

Grace Episcopal Church, photographed in 1912, was located adjacent to the Christian Science Church (the former James Tufts House), seen on the left. On the right is the Armory Prentice House, a Colonial revival mansion that was razed in 1934, and is today the site of the Regency and the Regal Condominiums. (Courtesy of the Medford Historical Society.)

The First Baptist Church was built in 1842 on Salem Street, adjacent to the Salem Street Burial Ground. Used until 1872, when a new church was built on Oakland Street, it later became a livery stable owned by Charles Day, after which it was used for various purposes until it was demolished in 1940. (Courtesy of the Medford Historical Society.)

The First Methodist Church was built in 1845 at the corner of Salem and Oakland Streets. This simple Greek Revival meetinghouse was used until 1873 when a new church was built on Salem Street, opposite Tufts Street. (Courtesy of the Medford Historical Society.)

The Medford Universalist Church was built in 1832 on Forest Street, just north of the Bigelow Block. Founded in 1831, the first pastor was Reverend Einslow Wright. (Courtesy of the Medford Historical Society.)

The Mystic Congregational Church was built in 1875 at 30 Salem Street, just east of Forest Street. On the left is the old burying ground, and on the right the Francis House where "Medford Crackers" were first baked and Lydia Maria Child was born. Today used by the New England Baptist Church, its landmark spire was unfortunately removed just a few years ago. (Courtesy of the Medford Public Library.)

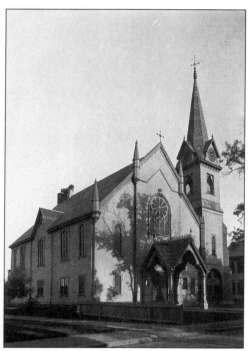

The Oakland Street Baptist Church was a large Stick-style church with a polychromatic slate roof and spire. This church burned in 1936 and its successor, the First Baptist Church, was built at 29 Oakland Street. A gracious Georgian church with monumental columns supporting a pediment, it is the third edifice of this resilient church. (Courtesy of the Medford Historical Society.)

The Methodist Episcopal Church was a large Stick-style church with a soaring polychromatic slate roof. It was built in 1873 on Salem Street, opposite Tufts Street. In 1900, the Methodist Episcopal Church built a church on Winthrop Street on the Hillside. That church was replaced by the present church in 1962. (Courtesy of the Medford Public Library.)

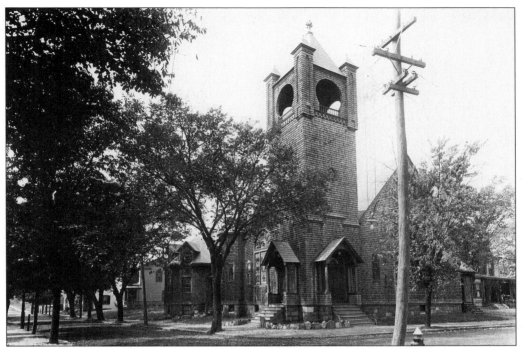

The West Medford Trinity Methodist Episcopalian Church (later the Shiloh Baptist Church) was a Shingle style church built in 1898 at the corner of Houlton and Bower Streets. (Courtesy of the Medford Historical Society.)

The West Medford Baptist Church was founded in 1895. The church was designed by Lewis H. Lovering in 1897 and was constructed at the corner of Boston Avenue and Harvard Street. (Courtesy of the Medford Historical Society.)

The Congregational Church of West Medford began just after the Civil War, worshipping in Mystic Hall on Harvard Avenue. The original church, which was used until a fire destroyed it in 1903, was built in 1873 on Harvard Avenue. The present stone church was built in 1904 on High Street, in a traditional English Gothic style with a square tower that has a four-sided clock. (Courtesy of the Congregational Church of West Medford.)

Saint Joseph's Church was designed by Thomas Houghton of Keeley & Houghton. The cornerstone was laid in 1893, but the church was not dedicated to Saint Joseph until 1912. An impressive Romanesque Revival design with a bell tower of 120 feet, it dominates High Street. Saint Joseph's Parish Hall was built on the site of the Magoun Estate. (Courtesy of the Medford Public Library.)

Saint Raphael's Church, designed by McGinnis and Walsh, was built in 1905 on High Street in West Medford. Built in the Spanish Mission Style so popular in the early 20th century, the church was destroyed by arson in 1990. The new church was designed by Dennis Keefe and was rebuilt in random laid stones that give the new church a modern feeling. (Courtesy of the Medford Public Library.)

Saint James Church was founded in 1920 to serve the Catholics of the Fellsway, Wellington, and Glenwood sections of Medford. Originally a small wood church, which was formerly a soldiers' barracks on Parker Hill in Roxbury, it was used until the present red brick church was built in 1927. Designed by Edward T.P. Graham (1871–1964,) it is an English Gothic design with an impressive Norman Tower. (Courtesy of Saint James Church.)

Saint Francis of Assisi Church was dedicated in 1930, serving the Catholics of the Fellsway and Fulton Heights neighborhoods. A stone church with French Gothic design, its spire is an interesting example of this style and can be seen from Interstate 93. A fourth church, Sacred Heart Church, was founded in 1937 at 51 Winthrop Street to serve the Catholics of Medford Hillside. (Courtesy of the Medford Public Library.)

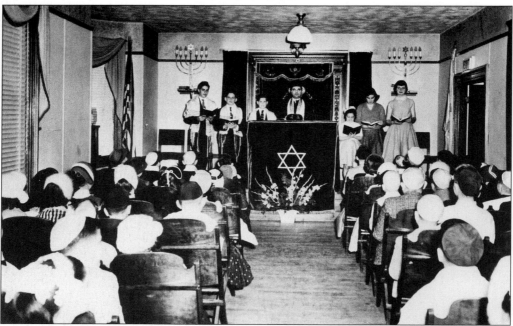

Services in the Medford Jewish Community Center and Temple Shalom were held at 42 Water Street from 1945 to 1958. Here, young adults on either side of the rabbi read from the Torah. Temple Shalom on Winthrop Street was designed by Perley F. Gilbert Associates and the first service was held there in 1958. (Courtesy of the Medford Historical Society.)

Seven

SHIPBUILDING

The *President* was built in 1850 at the shipyard of John Taylor, on Foster's Court. Commissioned by merchants William Bramhall and Thomas Howe of Boston, the ship had a tonnage of 1,021 1/2. This dramatic painting of the *President* was done by D. McFarlin in 1854. (Courtesy of the Medford Historical Society.)

Thatcher Magoun (1775–1856) is considered the "Pioneer Shipbuilder of Medford," and his first ship built in town was the brig *Mount Aetna*, built in 1803. From 1803 to 1836, Magoun built 84 vessels at his shipyard on Ship (now Riverside) Avenue, opposite Park Street.

The *Phantom* was built in 1852 at the shipyard of Samuel Lapham. It weighed 1,174 tons, and was among the 26 "blue ribbon" ships of the American merchant marine in the mid-19th century. The *Phantom* achieved a world's record by sailing from Callao to Rio Janeiro in 32 days. (Courtesy of the Medford Historical Society.)

When this picture was taken, shipbuilding had not changed since the early years, except that the ships were larger. Here two workers are standing on staging that surrounds a ship being built at the Curtis Yard on Union Street. (Courtesy of the Medford Public Library.)

A ship on stacks is readied for launching in 1868 from Foster's Shipyard, located on Foster Court off Riverside Avenue. With flags flying in the wind, the ship would be gently eased into the Mystic River for completion. (Courtesy of the Medford Public Library.)

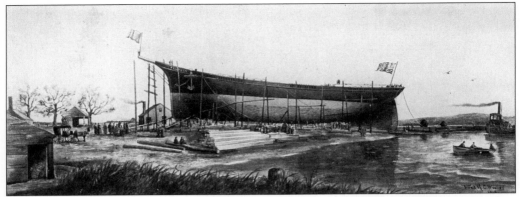

The ship *Pilgrim* lies ready for launching on December 4, 1873, at Foster's Shipyard. Built for Henry Hastings, this 956-ton ship was the last of all Medford-built ships to be launched into the Mystic River. (Courtesy of the Medford Historical Society.)

Joshua T. Foster (1810–1903) was a partner with John Taylor, their shipyard being the former Sprague & James yard on Foster's Court. After 1869, Foster operated the shipyard as sole proprietor, building 42 vessels, among them the *Pilgrim*, the very last ship built in Medford. He later served as a state representative from Medford and was a director of the Malden and Medford Gas Company.

The *Reporter* was built in 1853 by Paul Curtis at his yard at the junction of South and Curtis Streets. Commissioned by William Weld, whose "Black Horse" flag flies from the mast, he was a successful Boston merchant. The *Reporter* had a tonnage of 1,474 and was painted in 1858 by Eugene Grandin. (Courtesy of the Medford Historical Society.)

James O. Curtis established his shipyard off Swan Street in 1839, where he built 78 vessels. A civic-minded gentleman, Curtis took great interest in the schools and served as a member of the Spot Pond Water Commission, which supplied water to Medford.

The Mystic Boat Yard was located on the south side of Riverside Avenue, opposite Pleasant Street. Photographed about 1916, the area would later be developed for the Saltonstall Senior Apartments. (Courtesy of the Medford Public Library.)

The Mystic Boat Yard had piers that projected into the Mystic River. The piers protected small boats during the winter months. A three-masted schooner is anchored on the left—one of the last reminders of the glory days of shipbuilding on the Mystic River. (Courtesy of the Medford Public Library.)

Eight

THE FELLS AND THE GYPSY MOTH

A group of ladies enjoy the bucolic scenery of Wright's Pond, a man-made sheet of water from a dam, at the turn of the century. Just 5 miles north of Boston, the Fells are "all stony hills and table-lands, almost uninhabited, and of wonderful picturesqueness and wild, rugged beauty" said Sylvester Baxter in 1879. Initially known as Five Mile Wood, the natural beauty of the Middlesex Fells is no less impressive a century later. (Courtesy of the Medford Public Library.)

Elizur Wright (1804–1885) is often referred to as the "Father of the Middlesex Fells." He described the area as "a volcanic locality full of rocks, small trees, birds and glacial scratches—the school apparatus of Nature." A resident of Boston, he purchased a summer estate in 1862 on Forest Street in Medford and was an early proponent of using the forest for recreational and educational purposes.

A group of cows grazes on the banks of Wright's Pond at the turn of the century. The pond's name perpetuates Elizur Wright's involvement in the Middlesex Fells, and a stone tower known as the Wright Memorial was built after his death. A squat, square stone tower with a peaked roof, it was designed by Arthur A. Shurcliff, and can be seen to the left, nestled into the trees as one travels north along Interstate 93 at Roosevelt Circle.

Looking from Medford toward Pine Hill, the highest elevation in town, the bucolic scenery was impressive and invigorating. Pine Hill had been stripped of all trees for firewood during the Revolution, and in 1855 it was again stripped for use by the shipbuilders. By the late 19th century the reforested Pine Hill had undergone numerous changes but would remain an impressive vista.

The approach to Crystal Spring was a tree-lined pathway with soaring pine trees on either side of the road. The country aspect of the Fells is all the more remarkable, as it was so close to Boston.

An 81-foot high observatory, designed by Lyman Sise for Samuel C. Lawrence, was built in 1899 on Rams Horn Hill in the Middlesex Falls, where it afforded panoramic vistas of the natural beauty. The name of the hill is perpetuated in Ramshead Road, off Lawrence Road.

The Ravine Road led to Virginia Wood, named for the daughter of Fannie Foster Tudor. Virginia Tudor died at the age of 20 in Paris, and her mother donated a tract of land to the Trustees of Public Reservations in her memory. Virginia Wood, a pine and hemlock grove, was eventually made part of the Middlesex Fells in 1923.

Sylvester Baxter was the person to coin the name "The Fells" in an article that was published in the *Boston Herald* in 1879. The word "Fells" connotes a wild, hilly country, and Baxter joined the term with the county in which Medford was located—Middlesex.

Sylvester Baxter and his daughters rest on a rock in the Middlesex Fells after an afternoon of botanizing. In the late 19th century, the Middlesex Fells were a popular destination for members of the Medford Camera Club.

The gypsy moth caterpillar escaped from the experiment room of Leopold Trouvelot at 27 Myrtle Street in Medford. Trouvelot had begun experiments in the crossing of silk worms and gypsy moths, hoping to breed a hybrid that would flourish in New England. However, after his experiments escaped, the caterpillar would wrought havoc on New England, with deforestation of entire communities resulting as the pest ate every leaf in sight! Eventually, it was found that the only remedy was the use of a spray of arsenate of lead to control the moths. (Courtesy of the Medford Public Library.)

Workers began girdling on trees to try and combat the quick-paced growth and voracious appetite of the gypsy moth. From the time the caterpillar eggs are laid to the time they molt is but a short period, and once they fly from their nest, these moths could destroy an entire stand of trees in but a few weeks. (Courtesy of the Medford Public Library.)

Employees of General Samuel C. Lawrence, whose estate comprised the area now known as the "Lawrence Estates," treat egg clusters of gypsy moths in the forest just north of the city farm in 1905. These men, grouped into five gangs of seven men each, tried their best to combat the voracious caterpillars. (Courtesy of the Medford Public Library.)

If an infestation of the gypsy moth could prove at all interesting, it would be this photograph from 1905. Here 40 employees of Samuel C. Lawrence pose in the branches of twin elms as they remove moth clusters. The 400-acre Lawrence Estate was heavily infested with the gypsy moth, and ex-mayor Lawrence spent a tremendous sum of money to combat the growth of moth clusters before the moths molted. (Courtesy of the Medford Public Library.)

City employees spray trees on Purchase (now Winthrop) Street before the trees are attacked by the gypsy moth. The stone wall bounds the Puffer Estate, at the junction of High and Winthrop Streets. (Courtesy of the Medford Public Library.)

The gypsy moths had lain nests throughout the Middlesex Fells area by 1905. Here, city employees remove nests from trees on Salem Street with the hope of combating the spread of the gypsy and brown tail moths. (Courtesy of the Medford Public Library.)

Nine
MEDFORD BOAT CLUB

These three gentlemen seem to be passing a leisurely afternoon in the early 20th century on the Mystic River in Medford. This motor launch, flying the American flag, was a far cry from the sleek clipper ships that had been built in Medford during the mid-19th century, as pleasure craft became the boats of choice by the early 1900s. (Courtesy of the Medford Public Library.)

The Medford Boat Club's Boat House was on Mystic Lake in West Medford, between the first and second lakes. The first meeting of the club was in 1898, when Charles Baxter was unanimously elected the first president of the club. (Courtesy of the Medford Public Library.)

This photograph shows the new clubhouse of the Medford Boat Club in 1904. The club offered accommodations for 36 canoes and a place for socialization before and after boat races, as well as a starting place for those racing against competing boat clubs. (Courtesy of the Medford Public Library.)

The Floats and the Annex of the Medford Boat Club shows how popular the club was at the turn of the century. Within the decade after its founding, the membership in the Medford Boat Club had tripled. (Courtesy of the Medford Public Library.)

The "Club Four" of the Medford Boat Club was the winner of the 1902 American Championship that was held at Chatham on Cape Cod. From the left are Howard, Garland, Mather, and Hunter. (Courtesy of the Medford Public Library.)

Some of the club dories were photographed in 1905 on the Mystic Lakes. Notice the three men paddling a canoe on the left. (Courtesy of the Medford Public Library.)

The Medford Boat Club also had members who kept ice boats that would be raced during the winter months. Here, standing on the frozen waters of the Mystic Lakes, members ready for an ice race in 1905. (Courtesy of the Medford Public Library.)

Ten

TRANSPORTATION

The arched bridge at West Medford was built in 1821 by Peter Chardon Brooks as a farm road to span the Middlesex Canal, which passed through his estate in West Medford. Photographed in the late 19th century, the canal had already been filled in, but the hammered granite arch still stood at High Street and Boston Avenue. (Courtesy of the Medford Public Library.)

Governor James Sullivan (1744–1808) served as governor of Massachusetts from 1807 to 1808. A prominent statesman, he was an integral part of the building of the Middlesex Canal, which was surveyed by Colonel Loammi Baldwin in 1793 and took ten years. The area where the canal ended at Charlestown was named Sullivan Square in his honor, and is today a major train and bus terminus.

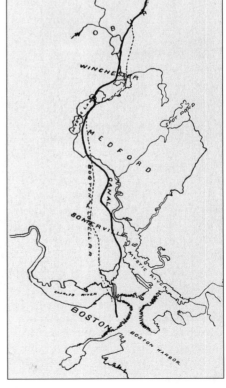

The Middlesex Canal ran from Sullivan Square at Charlestown to Lowell, connecting numerous towns by horse-drawn barges. Here, the canal ran through Medford along the Mystic River to South Street, where it veered west towards West Medford and north to Winchester and Woburn. Its charter was surrendered in 1852, after nearly five decades of service.

The rate of toll for items shipped by the Middlesex Canal was charged by the cargo's weight and the distance it was shipped.

RATE OF TOLL

ON THE

MIDDLESEX CANAL......UNTIL FURTHER NOTICE.

APRIL 4, 1808.

	Dolls Cts
ON all articles (excepting thoſe which follow) by weight at 6¼ cents a ton, each and every mile, the whole diſtance being 27 miles	1,68¾
Timber { Oak—per mile, 6¼ cents a ton	1,68¾
Timber { Pine—per mile. 4 cents	1,08
Pine Boards / Pine Plank, reduced to board meaſure } 6¼ cents	1,68¾
Clapboards—4 cents a thouſand	1,08
do. freight in the Proprietors' Boats—64 cents a thouſand	
Shingles—1 cent a thouſand	
Oak Plank, 2½ inch—6¼ cents for 600 feet board meaſure	1,68¾
Aſh Plank, 2½ inch—6¼ cents for 700 feet board meaſure	1,68¾
Staves, Barrel—6 cents per thouſand	1,62
do. Hogſhead—12 cents	3,24
do. Pipe—18 cents	4,86
do. Butt—25 cents	6,75
Hoops, Hogſhead—8 cents per thouſand	

Engine Number 471 of the Boston and Maine Railroad stands just outside the Engine House on Riverside Avenue. The spur from Medford Square to the main branch of the Boston and Maine Railroad was laid in 1845 and it induced real estate development throughout the 19th century. The granite wall on the right is part of the Salem Street Burying Ground. (Courtesy of the Medford Public Library.)

The College Hill Depot served the Medford Hillside and Tufts College not only as a depot, but as the post office for the college. Charles Foster, the station agent, and his daughter Nellie Foster, the postmistress, lived in the residential portion of the building. Notice the horse-drawn delivery wagon passing on Boston Avenue. (Courtesy of the Medford Public Library.)

The Boston and Lowell train passes Medford Hillside in the late 19th century. (Courtesy of the Medford Historical Society.)

Washington Street was the site of the Park Street Depot, located on the Medford spur that connected Medford Square and the main branch of the Boston and Maine Railroad. The bridge spanning Park Street can be seen in the distance. The Victorian houses were built in the area due to the convenience of transportation to Boston. (Courtesy of the Medford Historical Society.)

The Park Street Depot was photographed just prior to World War I. A handsome red brick and rough-hewn granite depot, it had a sloping slate roof with a large waiting room and ticket office. The depot, though on Magoun Avenue, was called the Park Street Depot. No longer used as a depot, it awaits reuse. (Courtesy of the Medford Historical Society.)

The West Medford Depot was on High Street at the square. A stone depot, it had a long sloping roof of slate with terra cotta ridge caps. A cupola surmounted the roof and was capped with a weathervane in the motif of a train. (Courtesy of the Medford Historical Society.)

This weathervane of a locomotive and coal car once graced the cupola of the West Medford Depot. After seven decades of dedicated weather-related service, it was acquired by the Henry Ford Museum in Dearborn, Michigan. (Courtesy of the Medford Public Library.)

A horse-drawn streetcar pauses in front of the Thomas Seccomb House in Medford Square about 1880. The first horse-drawn omnibus in Medford was the "Governor Brooks," which was run between Medford and Boston by Joseph Wyman beginning in 1805. Horse-drawn streetcars, which ran on a rail, replaced the omnibuses by the mid-1850s.

A horse-drawn streetcar passes the Thomas Seccomb House in the summer of 1900, as police officer Theiler looks toward the camera. The canvas shades are pulled up on the streetcar and the open sides must have offered a pleasant ride from Medford to Winchester and Woburn. (Courtesy of the Medford Historical Society.)

A horse-drawn streetcar approaches Puffers Corners (now Winthrop Square) from Purchase (now Winthrop) Street in 1896. This line, the N.W. Street Rail Road, connected Medford, Winchester, and Woburn. A horse-drawn wagon heads west on High Street on the right. (Courtesy of the Medford Historical Society.)

An electric streetcar passes a house on Boston Avenue near the bridge spanning the Mystic River. The route of this streetcar was listed as "Medford Hillside-Broadway-Winter Hill." (Courtesy of the Medford Historical Society.)

In this bucolic view taken in the spring of 1897, we see the first section of the Salem Street carhouse that opened in August of 1894. Later expansion of the carhouse lead to the demolition of the handsome tree-shaded house on the right. (Collection of Frank Cheney.)

This is a view of the busy Salem Street carhouse in 1909. Located on Salem Street near the Fellsway, this facility maintained the trolleys serving all of Medford and most of Malden. It was demolished in 1955. The site today is occupied by an MBTA bus garage and a shopping mall. (Collection of Frank Cheney.)

The intersection of Salem Street with the Fellsway was a busy junction for Medford's transit lines. In this June 1925 view looking down Salem Street from the Fellsway, a busy work crew is replacing worn streetcar track while a detail policeman watches. Both motor-driven and horse-drawn traffic passes the intersection. (Collection of Frank Cheney.)

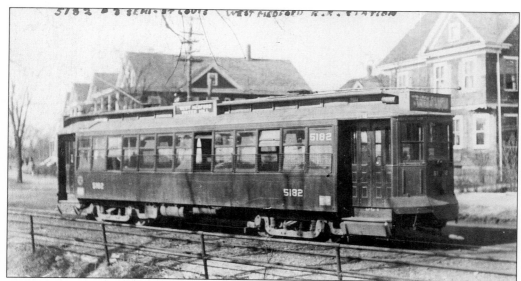

If you were a West Medford resident in the early 1920s, you reached downtown Boston by taking the trolley to Sullivan Square and then the Elevated to town. Here we see a car at the West Medford Railroad Depot (behind us) arriving from Sullivan Square. (Collection of Frank Cheney.)

Medford's handsome parkway is known as the Fellsway, and it once accommodated the trolleys of both the Boston Elevated and the Eastern Massachusetts Railway Companies. Here is an Eastern Massachusetts Railway car en route to Stoneham at Roosevelt Circle on the Fellsway in May of 1946. (Collection of Frank Cheney.)

On December 19, 1920, an Eastern Massachusetts Railway trolley en route to Sullivan Square from Reading and Stoneham pauses on the Fellsway at Fulton Street—without an automobile in sight! (Collection of Frank Cheney.)

Looking along Boston Avenue at Parallel Street on a foggy spring morning in 1932 is a Boston Elevated bus awaiting its scheduled departure time for Medford Square. The first motor buses in Medford began operations in May of 1923. (Collection of Frank Cheney.)

Between 1947 and 1959, riders on the Sullivan Square-Medford Square-Salem Street route were carried in quiet, fume-free electric trolley buses like the one seen here at Salem Street. While widely used in the Boston area, this was Medford's only electric bus route. (Collection of Frank Cheney.)

Eleven
LAWRENCE MEMORIAL
HOSPITAL

Members of the 1938 graduating class of the School of Nursing at the Lawrence Memorial Hospital pose for their photograph while holding bouquets of red roses. The hospital was founded through the bequest of Daniel Warren Lawrence (1830–1921), and its first president was Roswell Bigelow Lawrence (1856–1921). Incorporated in 1921 and opened on April 1, 1924, the Lawrence Memorial Hospital will celebrate its 75th anniversary in 1999. (Courtesy of the Lawrence Memorial Hospital.)

The Medford Visiting Nurse Association was founded in 1902 to provide care for those with medical needs in their own homes. Here, "visiting nurse" Mrs. Oakes rides her bicycle, which she used to make her round of house calls. Prior to 1921, the Peckham Hospital at Woburn and Allston Streets, and the Medford Hospital on Magoun Avenue were the only places available for patients requiring medical attention.

The Lawrence Memorial Hospital was built on 8 acres of land donated by Caroline Badger Lawrence, the widow of Samuel C. Lawrence. The facade of the new hospital was completed in 1924 and opened to provide medical assistance to all who required it. A nurse's home was built in 1925 and was enlarged five years later. In 1977, a two-story addition was built to better serve patients. (Courtesy of the Medford Public Library.)

Nurses and nursing assistants pose for their photograph in front of the Lawrence Memorial Hospital in 1932. The original Lawrence gift of 8 acres was added to by local businessman Andrew Curtin, who donated a strip of adjacent land. Lena Ivers Johnston was the first superintendent and administrator of the Lawrence Memorial Hospital School of Nursing, serving from 1923 to 1960. (Courtesy of the Medford Public Library.)

Onata Munsey, R.N. (on the right) instructs nursing student Ellen Kronquist in the preparation and correct folding of bandages. (Courtesy of the Lawrence Memorial Hospital.)

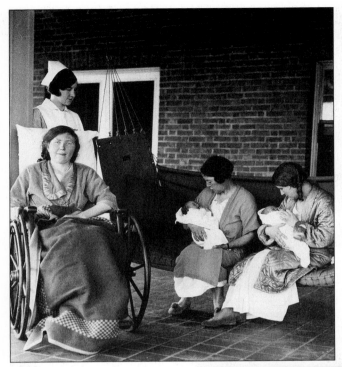

Patients resting on the roof garden of the Lawrence Memorial Hospital in 1925 are, from left to right: Miss Mary Conroy, Mrs. Mary Conway Sheehan (with her newborn), and Mrs. Luthera Woodward (with her newborn). Standing on the left is Ellen Kronquist, a student nurse. (Courtesy of the Lawrence Memorial Hospital.)

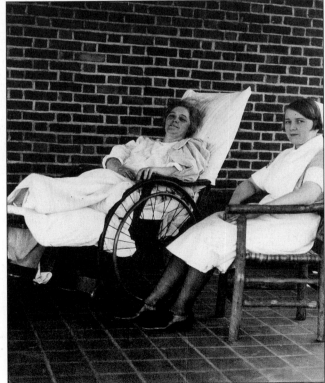

Mrs. Margaret Brown rests in a wheelchair on the roof garden at the Lawrence Memorial Hospital in 1925. Mildred Welch, a student nurse, keeps her company. (Courtesy of the Lawrence Memorial Hospital.)

Participating in an awards ceremony in 1947 are, from left to right: Gertrude Powers-Glade, Peg Leary, Alice Lyng, Sally Cronin, Ruth Gilman, Kay O'Brien, Kay Kelly, June Stead, Marion Bishop, Lorraine Cunning, and Lena Johnston. (Courtesy of the Lawrence Memorial Hospital.)

The Lawrence Memorial Hospital trained volunteer nurse's aides to assist the overworked nurses during World War II. Here, graduates of the program pose for their group photograph in 1945. (Courtesy of the Lawrence Memorial Hospital.)

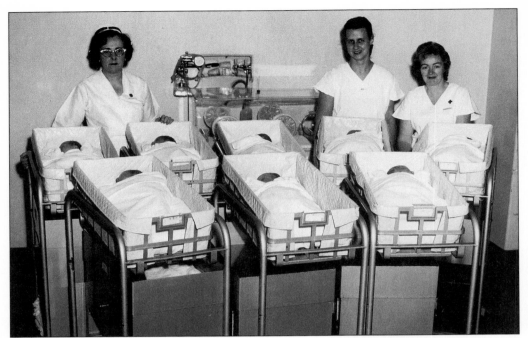

Eight babies were born at the Lawrence Memorial Hospital between December 20 and December 21, 1960. Standing from left to right are: Mabel Beyer, R.N.; Jessie Reinhart, nurse's aide; and Margo Griffin, R.N. The babies are, in the front row, Baby Boy LaConte, Baby Girl Conserva, and Baby Boy Assartato; in the second row are Baby Boys McCarthy, Schirpke, and Stover, Baby Girl Webber, and Baby Boy Lloyd. (Courtesy of the Lawrence Memorial Hospital.)

Volunteers are a major part of the Lawrence Memorial Hospital. With a tray of crocheted Santas and a vase of flowers are, from left to right: Jackie McGillivray, Rosann DiSarcina, and Teresa Favuzza, of Diversional Activities. (Courtesy of the Lawrence Memorial Hospital.)

Twelve

MYSTIC AND COMBINATION PARKS

The excitement of horse racing was never more evident than in this turn-of-the-century photograph of "Ruth D." and "Miss Adbell" nearing the finish line at Mystic Park. While cheering spectators lined the railings, the racers would compete for prize cups and silver trophies.

Race-goers arrived by foot, on horses, or in fancy liveries to watch the races at Mystic Park. A policeman stands on the far left to ensure that all who enter the racetrack be forewarned that if they become rowdy or abusive they will be ejected. (Courtesy of the Medford Historical Society.)

The streetcar line that connected Charlestown and Medford Square ran along Main Street in South Medford. Here, passengers who just emerged from a streetcar walk towards the entrance gate at Mystic Park—with the hope of a winning bet! (Courtesy of the Medford Historical Society.)

The Judge's Stand at the Mystic Park Racecourse was a neo-Egyptian two-story structure with an open, four-sided platform where the judge could watch every aspect of the race. Notice the horses grazing on the left. (Courtesy of the Medford Historical Society.)

Standing behind the bleachers of the racetrack in 1885 is "Gentleman Jim" Golden, a well-known enthusiast of horse racing. Golden Avenue, which bisects the former Mystic Park, was named in his memory. (Courtesy of the Medford Historical Society.)

The stables, or "Golden's Row" as they were often referred to, were long one-story stables for the horses who raced at Mystic Park. Mystic Park was sold in 1903 for development, and after a few years of lying fallow, the former race course was cut through by new streets such as Billings, Bowen, Golden, Wright, Alexander, Bonner, Mayberry, Willard, Pierce, Willis, and Rice Avenues and Harvard Street. The new avenues were named after the owners of the horses raced at Mystic Park. (Courtesy of the Medford Historical Society.)

Race-goers arriving in South Medford would see an almost rural area of the city; here at the corner of Main Street and Harvard Avenue about 1903, the Boynton Block (379 Main Street) can be seen on the left with the Medford House on the right. (Courtesy of the Medford Historical Society.)

The Medford House still stands on Main Street near the corner of Wright Avenue. It offered not only rooms to travelers but well-prepared meals for those who were not staying the night. Many who visited the Mystic Park races stayed, or dined, here. (Courtesy of the Medford Historical Society.)

Combination Park was a second race course in Medford, near the Somerville line on Mystic Avenue. Here, three drivers race their horse-drawn sulkies to the finish line. On the left can be seen a portion of the grandstand and the stables in the distance.

The stables at Combination Park created an area where horses could be walked between "heats," or races. Combination Park had a short life—opened in 1896, it was sold in 1901 for development.

Thirteen

TUFTS COLLEGE

Tufts College was founded as a Universalist college on the Walnut Tree Hill farm of Charles Tufts for "those young men who are obliged, on account of limited means, to struggle for their education." With Tufts' gift of land augmented by Timothy Cotting (1794–1872) of Medford, the campus grew so large that it was partly in Medford and partly in Somerville.

Charles Tufts (1781–1876) was a farmer and brickmaker who, through his generosity of donating land, was considered the founder of Tufts College. Donating a large portion of his farm on Walnut Tree Hill, he said he would "put a light on it," and the Universalist college was founded. Tufts served as a trustee of Tufts College from 1856 to 1876. (Courtesy of the Medford Public Library.)

Ballou Hall was named in honor of Reverend Hosea Ballou. Built in 1852–1853 as an Italianate red brick and sandstone building, it had recitation rooms, a dormitory, and bathing accommodations in addition to a chapel, library, and two literary societies. (Courtesy of the Medford Public Library.)

Reverend Hosea Ballou II (1796–1861) was the first president of Tufts College. Former pastor of the First Church in Medford, and grand-nephew of the famous Universalist Hosea Ballou, he was a well-respected minister who devoted the rest of his life to Tufts College after becoming president.

The Mystic Reservoir, part of the Mystic Water Works, was located at the top of Walnut Tree Hill. The campus of Tufts College was just beyond. From the left is the East Main Hall, the Gate House, West Hall, Main Hall, and the Barnum Museum. (Courtesy of the Medford Public Library.)

Goddard Chapel at Tufts was donated by Mary T. Goddard as a memorial chapel in honor of her husband, a former trustee and benefactor of the college. Designed by J. Philip Rinn of Boston, in the late 19th century the edifice was considered as "one of the ten finest pieces of architecture in New England." On the left, just beyond the trees, is Ballou Hall. (Courtesy of the Medford Public Library.)

Thomas Austin Goddard (1811–1867) was a trustee of Tufts College from 1856 to 1868. Goddard Chapel was built, through the generosity of Mary T. Goddard, his widow, in the style of a Romanesque chapel with a Lombardic tower. Mrs. Goddard also provided the funds for the gymnasium, built in 1884.

The Barnum Museum at Tufts College was donated in 1883 by Phineas Taylor (P.T.) Barnum, a trustee from 1852 to 1857. Barnum also presented a collection of stuffed animals, among them Jumbo—a stuffed elephant that had once been a part of the "Barnum and Bailey's Greatest Show on Earth." Jumbo, though destroyed in a fire in 1975, is still the mascot of Tufts College. (Courtesy of the Medford Public Library.)

Miner and Paige Halls were two early dormitories at Tufts College. Miner Hall was named in memory of Reverend Alonzo Ames Miner, president of the college from 1861 to 1875, and Paige Hall was named in memory of Lucius Robinson Paige, a former trustee of Tufts College. In 1955, Tufts took the necessary steps to change the school's name to Tufts University.

Fannie Merritt Farmer (1857–1915), on the right, was the famous author of *The Fannie Farmer Cookbook*, the "Bible" of cooks everywhere. A resident of Medford, her house was at the corner of Salem and Almont Streets. She became a legend in her own time for her recipes and cooking classes. Her cooking school, known as the Boston Cooking School, was not only popular, but would standardize the weights and measurements in recipes. (Courtesy of The Boston Athenaeum.)

Acknowledgments

Without the interest and assistance of Barbara Kerr of the Medford Public Library and Michael Bradford of the Medford Historical Society, this book would not have been possible. Their interest and generosity of their time is greatly appreciated. I would also like to thank the following for their interest and continued support:

Director Brian Boutilier of the Medford Public Library, Paul and Helen Graham Buchanan, Jamie Carter, Frank Cheney, Pat and Lucy Giannelli Catino, Janet Davenport, Dexter, Angela Giannelli, Carol Giannelli, Fred and Dolores Agri Giannelli, Joseph and Mildred Carvotta Giannelli, Louis and Mary Giannelli, Ralph Giannelli, Robert and Lucille Giannelli Gumbleton, Edward Gordon, Sheri Kelley (Tufts University Archives), James Z. Kyprianos, the Lawrence Memorial Hospital of Medford, Reverend Scotty and Ellen McLennan, the Medford Historical Society, Susan W. Paine, the late Stephen D. Paine, Reverend Michael Parise, the Pistone family, Dennis Ryan, Anthony and Mary Mitchell Sammarco, Gilda Sammarco, the late Joseph Sammarco, the late Luigi and Rose Giannelli Sammarco, Rosemary Sammarco, Sylvia Sandeen, Robert Bayard Severy, Gayle Sommer, my editor Amy Sutton, Reverend Larry Titus, William Varrell, and the Victorian Society, New England Chapter.